Families

Parents
Revised Edition

Rebecca Rissman

Heinemann Library
Chicago, Illinois

www.capstonepub.com
Visit our website to find out more information about Heinemann-Raintree books.

To order:

☎ Phone 800-747-4992

🖥 Visit www.capstonepub.com to browse our catalog and order online.

Edited by Rebecca Rissman and Catherine Veitch
Designed by Ryan Frieson
Picture research by Tracy Cummins
Originated by Capstone Global Library Ltd

Library of Congress Cataloging-in-Publication Data is available on the Library of Congress website.
ISBN 9781484668337 (pb)

Acknowledgments
We would like to thank the following for permission to reproduce photographs: Agefotostock: Picture Partners, 6; Alamy: Design Pics Inc, 17, 23; Getty Images: Asia Images Group, 18, AzmanL, 11, Ben Bloom, 7, Catherine Ledner, 19, Jasmin Merdan, 4, Jay Yuno, 5, SolStock, cover, Terry Vine, 13, Wang Leng, 10, 23; iStockphoto: Alexander Shalamov, 20, 23, Diane Labombarbe, 22; Shutterstock: BlueOrange Studio, back cover, 14, Dean Drobot, 9, Jacob Lund, 21, Kzenon, 16, 23, Monkey Business Images, 12, Olga Lyubkin, 8, Rob Marmion, 15

We would like to thank Anne Pezalla and Nancy Harris for their invaluable help in the preparation of this book.

Every effort has been made to contact copyright holders of any material reproduced in this book. Any omissions will be rectified in subsequent printings if notice is given to the publisher.

Contents

What Is a Family?

A family is a group of people.

The people in a family care for each other.

All families are different.

All families are special.

What Are Families Like?

Some families like to be active.

They like to play sports.

Some families like to be quiet.

They like to read books.

Different Parents

Parents are adults who have children.

Parents can be male or female.

Male parents are called fathers.

Some children call their fathers "Dad."

Female parents are called mothers.
Some children call their mothers "Mom."

Some families have two parents.
Some families have one parent.

Some families do not have parents.
Other adults help care for the children.

Sometimes parents remarry.
Sometimes they become stepparents.

Stepparents care for the children of other parents.

Many parents live with their children.

Some parents live apart from
their children.

Some parents adopt children.
The children join a new family.

Are there parents in your family?

Family Tree

Mother —— Father

You

Picture Glossary

adopt join a new family.
Many families adopt children.

adult grown-up

remarry get married again.
Many parents remarry.

stepparent grown-up that cares for children of other parents

Index

Note to Parents and Teachers

Before Reading

Explain to children that a family is a group of people who care for one another. Families can be very different. Most families include parents who care for the children. Some families have two parents, some have one parent, and some families include stepparents. Other families do not include parents. Other adults care for the children.

After Reading

• Talk to children about adoption. Explain that when parents adopt a child, they invite the child into their home to live. Some parents adopt one child. Other parents adopt more than one child.

• Ask children to draw a picture of their family and label the people in their drawing. Put these drawings up on display for everyone to enjoy!